Белой Горячки

Галлюцинации очень возможны.

Brain Fever #1

Publisher
Gene Yu

Editor
Mike Goodman

Production
Kathleen Ng

Correspondence
c/o Matchlock Press
PO Box 90606
Brooklyn, NY 11209
brainfever@matchlock.com

Contents

Brain Fever Vol. 1, No. 1, Spring 2017 (ISBN 978-1-939333-07-0) Version 1.0.
All contents copyright © 2017 by Matchlock Press except as follows: *Cadman Plaza* and *Subway Sketchbook* © 2015 by Agir; *Fruit Fast* © 2017 by Mike Goodman; *Eve's Temptation* and *Spectrum* © 2016 by Agir; *You Can't Get There From Here* © 2013 by Anicula; *To Land a Man* © 2017 by Olivia Schanzer; *Why We Occupy* © 2012 by Olivia Schanzer and Gene Yu; *Ballpoint Perps* © 2017 by Vava. The images on page 76 were derived from *Day 21 Occupy Wall Street October 6 2011 Shankbone 40*, by David Shankbone, which is licensed under the Creative Commons Attribution 3.0 Unported License.

To all you beautiful folks out there, I'm pleased to make your acquaintance! & if I know you already, I say 'hey' to you, too! & two kisses!

Some time ago a good friend of mine came to tell me that he was retiring. The man's in good health, nothing wrong with him at all. Good memory, working legs. From my end, nothing hoists the red flags more. Unless you're the cat in charge of the water buckets at Gitmo, it's the last thing you should do. & it *is* the last thing you *will* do! Retirement & high-fructose corn syrup are subsidized death! (Get that word out! & stop drinking Coca Cola!)

I don't say this from ego (though I've got one, same as anyone) but I'm not the type to let folks mess themselves up. I've gotten that phone call more than once: "Mike, it's me. I've taken the whole bottle of Haldol." & I never didn't go over. I've stuck my fingers down those dumb assholes' throats myself once or twice while we waited for the ambulance. So we can't leave him idle, right? We've got to purge that entropy!

Here we have a little project before you, my friends. & I mean both old friends & young—I'm starting to dig on you young friends; I like the way you keep trying to shake it up. Not sure you're succeeding any better, but

EDITORIAL

I like how you keep working. Someone, maybe Voltaire, said something about the ratio of failure to success, & you'll have to work it out a lot more times with the cops before you get anywhere. Don't despair, though. The cats who've walked the road before, we're cheering you on. You look good, man, you really do. & to our beautiful Indian friends in North Dakota. To them especially!

So I'm paying out a ransom here. My friend told me to get down a few stories & share them. If you want to take that time, here's one of them. Or just skip ahead to the pictures. When you're looking at a piece of paper, no one's looking back at you, & that's how we like it. Kiss those trees that give you freedom because they're your ally, too. See how those bastards cover us from Google Earth! The lungs & conscience of our mother, Gaia!

But now picture Mike: teeth still one-hundred percent, politics clean & clear, compromise in front not behind, one kid, no clap, & I still had faith in the communists! & check out the pics drawn by hand! & of course, all my stories have some balling! & even if there wasn't balling, I'm going to throw some in anyway, for you all!

Let's keep moving forward! Let's love each other!

Mike

Fruit Fast

A Reminiscence
by Mike Goodman

My first wife and I didn't last long in the scheme of things. But you have to remember in those days even college boys might get hitched at twenty, right in the middle of college. So they could ball legally and still attend church with their head high? Yeah, probably. If you're young you can't even understand that, right? You might never even have had someone tell you to wait on it, unless you were raised by bible-thumpers. But you could be twenty and not even allowed to have a girl in your dorm room behind a closed door. Never seen a girl naked, never going to without the ring.

So we married when I was in college, and we split up around the time I came back from California. The trip to California had been some kind of a trial separation, and I didn't bring her and Josh because I almost just forgot about them. Not that Mimi and Josh were forgettable, mind you. I just forgot that they were mine, or my responsibility. That can tell you where my head was at.

After I came back, it was a real separation. I didn't want to sign no papers, she didn't want to sign no papers, but we weren't together any longer. We made peace about it sometime later. She remarried not soon after we did finally sign the papers, and she's been with the guy since then. But even with that, we weren't at peace for some time. They've been together forty years to our four, and Josh has called him

Dad since the beginning. I don't even mind; I wasn't even a human being until I turned fifty.

So I fucked up my marriage. I stood them up and ran off, but if you can believe these things, I was devastated when we actually split up. I felt like it was a decision that she and my mother made without any input from me whatsoever, and my mother and father were absolutely on her side about the whole thing. My father didn't talk to me for a year and a half after we separated, that's how pissed he was. He had a list of things to be pissed about, and was still complaining about my hair on his death bed, but the number one thing he couldn't let go was what happened with Mimi and Josh.

Now, I don't disagree with him, but he couldn't prioritize, and he acted like the way I put myself together was the same thing. In his mind it was the same thing. Dope, my long hair, what happened with Mimi. Now *I'm* a father, and obviously I don't give a shit about the state of my kids' hair, and I even don't give a shit about their relationship with dope. They're grown now and that's not my affair. But I would have something to say if I saw them torpedoing a relationship with someone they loved.

My ex went on living with my parents for several years, and my mother took care of my son while Mimi went back to work as a kindergarten teacher. Even after Mimi moved out she lived down the block from them for years, even after she remarried. When I was just running around tongue-deep in pussy and LSD, I liked to think of my crew-cutted dad with Josh on his knee, watching the game on Sundays. So I can't give it back to him for the lack of understanding; cosmically, he bailed my ass out where my kid was concerned.

So as I said, I was not acting sane, I was not processing. I had done something to myself, and then it was like the whole force of the universe had hurt me. I cried and cried; I don't even know in retrospect what I was crying for; it was like with Nixon, you just believed something, and then suddenly the facts changed and you weren't able to believe in it anymore. What I thought was going to happen? I guess I just thought that Mimi would be the sort of person who would wait for me, and it wasn't the case.

I was adjuncting at a community college nearby, and besides getting up and going to work, the majority of my time was spent smoking grass and lying in bed. I didn't grade papers, I just threw them in the trash, and when the kids asked me where their papers were I would always give them a nice long lecture about what was going on in the world and how unimportant their work was when you thought about old grandfathers getting napalmed, and what the SNCC kids were going through to get out the vote, and Silent Spring and the animals dying. To be honest I didn't think whether they got their papers back at all mattered at the time, and I'm not sure I do now.

I was offered a better job out west by a friend in the English department of a state school, a former advisor of mine, but I didn't accept the offer. This was just pure self-suppression, as the Scientologists say. That happened, and then there was a woman I liked a lot at the time after my wife, but I cut off that one too. I never even talked to her again, and I'd like to think that that one episode in her life was of no account, and she doesn't even remember me. But I remember her, and if I'm reminding her of me now—by some strange Karmic link-up, she's reading this—please, Tuesday, just forget it again.

So now you've got my scene. I'm on a self-sabotage death trip, wearing myself out with tears and self-pity and all kinds of recriminations, yet doing the same thing over and over again. I'm screwing up relationships. I don't give a shit about my job, or any other job I might get. I'm down for freedom and for the cause, but I'm not willing to lift one finger in helping anyone else out, because I'm too busy on my own bullshit. Go down to Mississippi? Sorry, I'm too busy crying in my beer because the woman I love left me when I asked her to!

After what I'd seen in California, it seemed like nothing was happening in the town where I lived. Just these isolated teenage types who'd ordered peyote buttons from mail-order catalogues. They'd stop me in the post office to tell me about their trips because my hair was an inch below my collar; but theirs was a personal freak-out only. I myself had gone out of my way that fall to isolate from any type of scene or community, and though I wore long hair and knew a few people who also smoked grass, my town wasn't crawling with people who had turned on.

However, there was this one group of folks who lived on an apple orchard up there. I think what happened was that it had been a working orchard run by regular people, a husband and wife, and they died suddenly, maybe in a car accident, I'm hazy on the details. Suddenly the farm was left to their children, a girl maybe twenty, and a boy who was probably sixteen or seventeen. Did you ever read Pippi Longstocking? My daughter was crazy about it back when.

This was what happened with the apple farm: Regular types who knew something about orchards were on them to sell, sell, sell, but the pair of them would have seen the farm go to shit before they sold it. Which is what happened. They didn't pick any of the apples beyond what they ate themselves, and they let the hired hands go and all the employees, or really they just stopped paying them so that they couldn't be bothered coming back. If you drove past it on the road that first fall, the smell of rotting apples was intense—not really a bad smell, but just intense.

Their neighbor who supplied the bees for fertilization came and did it for free, just to be a good neighbor and for the memory of the kids' parents. It was a good orchard, and it hurt all the neighbors to see what was happening to it, but the girl had inherited it fairly, and there was nothing they could do about it.

At some point, by invitation or not, teenagers from around the area would go to the orchards to hang out, and then it seemed they had even imported some big-city types who were a mix of ages. The second year, they started to pick the apples, and got back up their pick-your-own business, but all with a decidedly Freak sensibility and Freak vibe. Instead of nice, clean-shaven farmers on stepladders, you had stoned boys with no know-how whatsoever hanging off the branches like orangutans, just swinging there in the breeze.

I got to be a little friendly with Mary, the girl who owned the place, and one day I was in the post office mailing my electric bill. I'd been so depressed, I'd let them shut it off though I'd had money to pay. Now that fall was upon us, even I could see that shut-off electricity was not going to fly in the dead of winter. I was in an apartment over someone's garage, and couldn't make a go of it with a wood stove or like that. Anyway, I was in the post office and I saw Mary, who was there with some nice-looking teenage girl. I was in my mid-twenties myself, if you're asking about my tastes and proclivities.

The teenage girl saw that I was a friend of Mary's—or that Mary knew me, I don't know that we were friends—and she looked me over. My hair was just over my collar, which you modern cats would be surprised meant something in that place and time, though I was probably wearing a dress shirt and that kind of adjunct drag, and she started telling me all about the new plan at the orchard, and how they were "letting the poor people take as many apples as they wanted, just like Jesus," and that kind of thing. I asked Mary about this, and she said, "Aw, yeah, yeah, we couldn't let them go to waste like last year," and that some folks from the city had come up to help them. I asked them what they were doing about paying taxes and for food if they weren't making much money except around the edges—I was still a little on the straight and narrow then, or I still knew it was there—but

she said they weren't worrying about that. God provided, like in the Garden of Eden. The girl added then that they didn't need any other food; she had been living all summer with apples as her only source of sustenance. I called bullshit, but the teenage girl said no, she was telling the truth.

I'll tell you that something about this impressed me, and now you'll get a handle on my state of mind. I liked the teenage girl, who was lamming it from Brooklyn College and her parents. The kind of kid you were just starting to get all over the country: hitching, smoking dope, vagabond kind of girl. I was glad to get an invitation to go over and hang out with the people at the orchard. I was lonely back east because I couldn't connect with my old friends. Some of them had even gone to Vietnam of their own free will. Families like that. And my new friends were far away on the West Coast.

I went over that night, having no one to go home to and still having no contact with my wife, my son or even my parents, who were so burned about my behavior. Once, I saw my Dad in the grocery store and he wouldn't even say hi to me, that's how pissed he was. If you asked me now, I would say to my old self: "Leave town, Mike. Get out of there until you can get your head together." But I didn't do that until the following fall.

There was a whole group of people living in Mary's parents' house, and it was a queer thing as all the family stuff was still around, portraits of them all, and her mother's corny knickknacks, religious things. It was a sad thing to me at the time in my state of mind, because the mother and father were dead, and here were Pippi Longstocking and her horse just hanging out with their weirdo friends smoking grass in the living room on top of the mother's crocheted blankets. I never got over that feeling that the whole thing wasn't right, but they were nice kids, and it's not like they torched the place. They swept up, kept it clean.

I had my suspicions about the ones up from the city, that there was some kind of advantage being taken, but they seemed more to be taking care of Mary and her brother than taking advantage. Dinner that first night was this enormous apple pie that one of the city ladies had made, and it was a great dinner even though it got me down, thinking about Mary's mother and how she wouldn't have approved. And maybe I was even thinking that there was no point to any of it. That we should just take the whole thing as it was: Vietnam, and everyone kept down and in their places so that we would stop killing our parents and making them cry. I was really bummed out and paranoid from the grass; thoughts like this were just getting me going. I was thinking about

children and all the troubles of the world, and how the babies in Vietnam wanted someone to hold their little hands, too, but their dads were stuck in holes in the ground with AK-47s on their laps.

The man sitting next to me at the table—he was a wild-eyed, wild-haired Jewish cat, the kind I'd meet every foot at City; his name was David— remarked on my expression. He looked into my eyes and he said to me, "You okay, man?" something simple like that, "You want me to take you outside, get you some air?" I needed air, man. It was just like the knickknacks and the parents and these dumb kids were sitting on my chest, pressing all the air I had out of me.

I was so touched by this that I suddenly told him everything about my wife and my son and my heartache over our separation, even though I had caused it one hundred percent. He listened out on the porch, and then he thumped the floor and said, "I see that you're suffering, and I've got an answer for you, my friend. Just listen to what I have to say and don't say yes, don't say no. You need to clear your head and clean up your body. You have unhappiness and toxins flowing through you. I was pre-med at Columbia before I ended with all that, so I can tell you. You know how much Columbia has invested in napalm? I couldn't stay in a place like that. But you're sallow. You have dark circles under your eyes. You're underweight. I bet you can't get a good night sleep without a six pack of beer." This was the truth. I felt at that moment that this man had some real insight to offer. "You need a change, Mike." Here I was, ready to do anything he said. His confidence was just overtaking me. "Put yourself in my hands for one month, and I will have you feeling like a new man by the end of that time. At the end of the month, I promise you can have yourself back to do what you want."

I said, "Absolutely," without a further thought on the matter, and we shook on it. "You take over, man. I'm sick and tired of being in charge of this lump of shit."

"The first thing," said my new friend, "is you can't smoke a cigarette during that time. Can you do that?" I didn't think I could, and he said, "Okay. How about not more than five a day?" I still wouldn't agree, and he said, "Fine, just don't expect this to work as well.

"Then you need to drink one gallon of fresh water a day. Not less. You're getting the impurities out of your body."

"I can't drink that much before class. I have to be in there for an hour and a half at a time."

"Okay, fine. Don't drink before class, start it up after you leave class. Knock it off an hour or two beforehand." I agreed.

"What about coffee?"

"Coffee is fine," he said, "but there is one part of this that is non-negotiable. You're going to eat no food at all except for one. The food they sinned on in the Garden of Eden, Mike. God's food." I was ready to agree; I hardly had to hear more. "Look at Carol—" That was the teenager. "She's been living on apples alone for three months. Look how good she looks. She was a basket case before. She got kicked out of Brooklyn College because the doctor told her she was psychotic. Mike, she was in a mental hospital. She was a junky, a psychotic junky living on chocolate bars, and seeing—what'd you see all the time, Carol?"

"God," Carol called over.

"It wasn't really God, though. Because God does not distract you from your tasks and your life like that. God does not make you a gibbering lunatic who can't keep up with school. But now she's as sane as could be."

"That can't be true."

"It's true. Just try it, Mike. Clearly you have nothing to lose. You're already a total wreck. I haven't had another substance in six months, besides a hamburger once a week. That's a separate issue, though; I have to stay in touch with my animal side." You hear this, and you say: "Mike did not agree to try this plan." I'm in touch with you, and I hear you saying it. Nevertheless, I agreed to try his plan. David from the city offered me the use of the orchard juicer without restriction, and took me out to the orchard to give me two bushels of Mary's apples to put in the trunk of my 1953 Pontiac Chieftain. That was a helluva car, with this enormous straight-eight engine. What a cruiser! Made it across the country eight or nine times. I wish I had it now, but I traded it a while later to my buddy for a 1959 Volkswagen. So did everyone else!

"Better you should juice them," he said. "The less you use your teeth the better." Somehow this made sense to me, too. Other than the thing with the apples, the guy from the city seemed reasonable. He was taking history classes at the college, and when I asked a history professor I knew about him, the man had nothing but nice things to say.

"Marxist, hard-core," said the professor. "Good people." He had never mentioned the apples to the professor, who was a bit of a straight though he was down with the communists, and I didn't tell him, either. It was the kind of thing that was a great plan when you were with people who believed in it, but some part of you was sheepish about it, if you thought someone would argue.

After the first week, I felt my mood lift, though when I went on the scale I'd lost seven pounds, and I was already underweight at that time. You wouldn't think it to look at me now, but as a teenager I bought Charles Atlas from the back of the comic books; I drank raw eggs for breakfast. If I could wind my metabolism back up to the rate it was when I was a kid, I'd live forever. But I didn't care about the weight loss. I felt better and I let David know the next time I saw him.

"Of course you do. This is utterly scientific."

After the second week my state turned around again. I was queasy most of the time, and even more exhausted than I'd been before. David's response was: "You have to go through it to come out the other side."

The third week I had to ask a friend to cover my classes, and I could hardly get out of bed to go to the bathroom. In the fourth week, I lost a tooth. It just fell out, no pain or anything. I brought it to David to examine; for some reason it didn't occur to me to go to the dentist.

He shined a flashlight into my mouth, and looked around for some time. Finally he pronounced, "You need more water. You're dehydrated," and he added, "Now's not the time to lay off the apples." For some reason, this made complete sense to me, so much sense that I remember repeating it to myself like a mantra, "Mike, now's not the time to lay off the apples. Now's not the time to lay off the apples."

A few days after I lost the tooth, I got a second wind and my energy came back up. I went over to the apple farm to hang out, and found myself sitting downstairs with Carol, the friend of Mary's who was billed as psychotic, talking in the living room. One thing led to another, as it often did in those days, and I proposed the idea that we go upstairs to one of the bedrooms and make it. Carol agreed—she told me that she always liked me, she'd been thinking of it herself—and we went upstairs to what must have been the parents' old bedroom—more quilts, more framed family photos, more crochet. The closet door in there was ajar, and I looked in and just saw this row of really square dresses, dresses I'd never seen Mary in, that had to have been her mother's. Going-to-church dresses. I think there was even a hatbox at the top of the closet. So that didn't start well.

The girl and I took off our clothes and got under the quilts. All was going as it should, and then Carol said to me, "Boy, you've gotten skinny on all those apples." I laughed and I looked down, and I've got to say, I got a little nervous when I saw what I looked like. I hadn't really taken a serious look at my body recently—in those days I usually fell asleep in my jeans, and I didn't shower as much as I might have. I was a sight: concave chest, the whole thing, pelvis looking like a skeleton who walked right out of a grave. Carol and I both laughed nervously. She got a serious voice and said, "Mike, you should think about seeing a doctor. I don't know if you know it, but David isn't a real doctor. He got kicked out after a semester. He doesn't know anything about medicine." I didn't know what to reply to this. For some reason, when she said it, it seemed surprising to me.

You could tell she was a little turned off, and was only going forward with it so as not to hurt my feelings, but when I asked her if she wanted to stop, she said, "Not at all, not at all." And I wasn't going to stop just because my feelings were hurt.

So, we got into it. You know the way it goes, but I was definitely feeling more tired than I usually did. I mean, I was basically lying there and letting her do all the work. Not very good manners, by my own personal standards. Finally she asks, really concerned, worried about the whole thing, "Are you okay? Do you want me to stop?" I don't know what to answer. I'm so tired, suddenly I can't keep my eyes open, but I don't want to hurt her feelings, so I kind of mentally slap myself in the face. "Get it together, Mike!" that kind of thing.

So then I get on top. I've got to show her I'm into her, I'm not just wasting her time. I don't want to hurt her feelings, you see. That was part of my code then and now, a very important part of Karma, sexually speaking, especially when I was rambling and not just with one lady, like now. Maureen is used to my shit, and she doesn't feel anything about it, she tells me all the time.

Anyhow, I got on top. I was kind of pumping away. She seemed into it, etc., you know, doing what the ladies do when they like where you're at, when suddenly the sides of my vision start to cloud up, and boom! Everything goes black.

"What's wrong? What's wrong?" I heard faintly, and then, you know how these stories go, the next thing I knew, I was lying on that bed, stark naked, and David was hovering over me with a jam jar filled with juice, saying "Drink it, drink it." Also in the room was Carol—who had gotten dressed fully before going to get help, though she hadn't thought to even pull the blanket up over me—the girl and boy who owned the farm, and three or four of their friends up from the city. So I come to in this room crowded with freaks.

"Stay back and give the man air," David said, and all those heads didn't move an inch. David seemed like the sane one there. Two of them even sat down at the foot of the bed and passed a joint back and forth between them.

"What's the smell?" I finally asked when I found my tongue. I didn't drink the juice, I just somehow gummed my dry tongue until it got moisture back. "What's on me?" I felt my body. The lower half was covered in a sticky substance, unlike anything I knew. It was thin liquid that had dried. It wasn't piss. It wasn't cum.

"My friend," said David gently, "that is from your own body. You have just passed into the final stage of your fast, for you have spontaneously ejaculated apple juice! Your own body made it!" He seemed delighted, and for a moment of clarity, I saw him and his wigged-out hair. He was not a kindly country doctor of the hippie persuasion. He was a demented Doctor Frankenstein.

"It's true," squealed Carol. "As you were falling over, it just came out! Apple juice, Mike!" Carol seemed more shaken than David, but there was a note in her voice—I can still hear it now—that registered. This girl is psychotic. The people smoking the joint at the foot of the bed shook their heads. They did not seem convinced any of this was a good thing. The guy on the right there patted my foot and said, "Rough stuff, man. Rough stuff." He went back downstairs, and came back about ten minutes later with a cheese sandwich—processed cheese, processed bread, mayonnaise. It was the most delicious meal of my entire life, up 'til then or after. Even still, though we eat macrobiotic at home, I sometimes buy Wonder Bread and American cheese and hide it at the back of the refrigerator. Thanks to the anonymous head who supplied me that day!

Since then I've never eaten another apple. Not one. When asked, I say I'm allergic. I even told that to a doctor once during a checkup. He asked about allergies, and I said I have anaphylaxis from apples. He said, "How do you know?" and I said, "That's what my mother told me."

It took me another year to feel better about my divorce, and so the apples did nothing on that front either, except that they gave me a worse problem to distract me. That works. If you've ever heard that Yiddish story: A poor guy has a full house, eight kids, a mother-in-law, and he goes to the rabbi to find out what to do about all the fighting. The rabbi tells him to bring all the farm animals into his house and live with them. Then, when things are as bad as they can be, he tells him to take them all out. This leaves him only with his fighting family, which seems okay, now that the animals have gone. For me, once I was no longer ejaculating apple juice, things didn't look so bad.

This was only one of my reckless experiments in those days. For instance, the summer before I met the apple farmers, I dropped acid every day in the hopes of changing my outlook. If you do the math on that, it's about 200 micrograms a day for approximately 90 days. So maybe I was a little softened up for the juice fast already. Hard to say. ℰ

I SHOULD BE FLATTERED, I GUESS.

TO THINK THAT THESE YOUNG GIRLS MIGHT STILL TAKE AN INTEREST IN ME!

MAYBE THIS IS AN ELABORATE PLOY DESIGNED TO BOOST MY SELF-ESTEEM.

SNORT! THAT'S A GOOD ONE!

YOU DON'T THINK SHE WOULD DO THAT FOR ME?

I WOULDN'T HAVE THOUGHT YOU WORTH THE EFFORT.

BUT THIS NEW, MORE MATURE, REFLECTIVE RICO SHOWS PROMISE.

DON'T YOU MEAN THIS MORE DOCILE, DOMESTIC, WHIPPED RICO?

THAT'S *YOUR* HANGUP, NOT MINE!

YOU KNOW, I MIGHT BE DOOMED TO FALL SHORT, BUT I STILL WISH I KNEW WHAT KIND OF MAN SHE REALLY WOULD WANT ME TO BE.

NEXT: "COUNCILMAN SIEFERT"

You Can't Get There From Here

An Essay
by Anicula

IT is a surprised eye that notices, while watching an episode of *Sesame Street* from 1969, the pieces of trash in the gutters. It's a set, after all. The trash could not have simply appeared the way that real trash does in real gutters. Instead, we can assume a hand has laid it there purposefully, in gutters that the hand, or one like it, has also constructed.

The walls are distressed, too, in the way you do the old railyards of a miniature train set, and probably using the same materials: Rust is added, paint applied and then chipped. The shops are brown-tinged and broken down. Light-bulbs hang bare from the ceilings.

You can imagine the team of hippie technicians, their beards sweaty and full of paint flecks, down on their hands and knees applying Insta-Rust, or scouring nearby dumpsters for the right old wooden boards to incorporate into the wall outside Big Bird's alley. The whole thing is an extremely careful and well-considered simulacrum of a poor neighborhood— a project that wouldn't seem to go along with the production of a children's television show, and certainly hadn't up until that point.

The naturalism—a funny word to use about a show that features Snuffleupagus periodically lumbering through—extends beyond the set to a predominantly black and Hispanic cast that represents the demographics of a poor neighborhood, and whose behavior warmly echoes that of real residents. Maria is often found reading on her fire escape, maybe avoiding the heat of her apartment or enjoying the one outdoor space available to her. David too can be found on his building's ledge, sometimes listening to his transistor radio. Bert and Ernie live in a basement apartment behind garbage cans. Luis's repair shop specializes in the patch-up jobs of people who can't easily afford to replace items like clock radios.

The show feels remarkably gritty to a modern viewer. Even if you watched it as a kid, those rough edges are surprising. The environment hews too closely to its sources not to have a faint odor of melancholy, and you might imagine that odor being ratings death in another production's hands.

Still, the show is enormously cheerful. The cheer doesn't come from the context, though, but from the people, monsters and animals who live in it. There are neighborhood-wide games of follow-the-leader, parades, and *ad hoc* marching bands, with people picking up the lids of trash cans on which to beat time. (There is a surprising amount of interaction with trash cans for a viewer from our own germ-phobic times, and children seem to go out of their way to sit on or hit the tops each time they pass. A modern mother might be forgiven for holding down the nearest child as a proxy, and decontaminating him.) Cookie Monster gorges on cookies and leaves behind a trail of pleasant crumbs. Balloons are frequently carried, and fruit is shared. Songs are sung with the cast; cows, people, children and monsters joining in. It is to be noted that a great deal of the enjoyment comes from the children on the show. (The children, pointedly, are not trained, and are as awkward and unschooled as any other delightful group of kids at their performances.) Plans are made. Someone is always picking up to go somewhere, and inviting others along, though we only hear about it; we never follow them where they are going.

The outside world beyond the set is incorporated only in short movies. There are scenes of the countryside, farms and rural life, and amazing shorts of an Appalachia that in the sixties and seventies was right on the verge of upending social change, but still, for the moment, had its folkways. Men in 1950s ducktails and short-sleeved button-downs build stools and deliver the mail on horseback, all against a background of bluegrass music. We are shown zoos and places of business, too. Through these movies, small viewers can discover what's beyond their neighborhoods, what jobs are out there, where people live. They are encouraged in the luxury and necessity of dreams as they are kept grounded in a reality that they really do occupy. The clear message of the show is: "You can get there from here."

This is a message heard often by children, and often espoused in children's media and in schools. It is a crucial message for poor children—for any children—to hear, but so often it seems baldly disingenuous. In the early episodes of *Sesame Street*, the difference was that the creators understood and reflected back to the viewers where the

Sesame Street is an extremely careful and well-considered simulacrum of a poor neighborhood.

here of poor children actually was. Because of this overt presentation there was no stigma; a child was free to play, aspire, and dream openly. After all, Bert and Ernie seemed to be poor, too.

If all this seems peculiar to us now, it's because *Sesame Street* was born in the distant and alien context just after LBJ declared his war on poverty, a time not at all like ours. Initially it was funded by Head Start, a program still around today, a product of that Johnson initiative. The Head Start program was committed to helping kids get a leg up before school started, and the show was planned to enhance that. The idea that poor children might be enfranchised, and the problem of poverty solved, by throwing money at their educations is today an idea that sounds suspiciously utopian. But brilliant people and the fat wallet of a flush federal government were of a like mind on the question of children and their families.

In 1969, poverty rates for whites in New York City ran parallel to the rest of the country. The national average of 13.7% was reflected in the city's overall average of 14.5%. But the citywide average for Hispanics of 27.9% and for blacks of 23.7% clearly put children from those communities at a disproportionate disadvantage.[1]

Just like Head Start, the goal of the Children's Television Network was to lessen the gap between poor and middle class children by helping them to prepare for school in the way that the more affluent parents did. The creation of shows that would do that was approached scientifically by educators who steered things, testing the shows extensively before target audiences. It seems unlikely that such a methodological approach would have achieved such organic fare, but it did. The massive bureaucracy behind the show remains invisible in the end product, with the only hints that the show has been labored over appearing in the wide range of animation, songs, puppets, movies and sequences in each show, and in the sense of depth present in all these things. This is a feeling that even small children can pick up on.

Reading readiness and numeracy—skill building—was only one focus of the show. After all, new ideas about the emotional and moral life of children were just becoming widespread in education circles; the open secret that kids were people in and of themselves and should be handled accordingly was at the very least filtering down into the consciousnesses of even the most benighted teachers.

Great care was taken to address the emotional needs of the viewers. The adults and puppets functioned as stand-in family members, and the expression of love, caring and concern was paramount, though not maybe in the way we are used to seeing it expressed now.

There was an unselfconscious free flow to the interactions between the puppets and the children: gentle teasing when answers were gotten wrong, lectures on off behavior. In one segment, Kermit asks a little girl to recite the ABCs with him. As she does it, she keeps breaking up her progress through the alphabet: "A, B, C, D, Cookie Monster," she says, and goes into repeated gales of laughter. Kermit gets more and more frustrated with her. "Cookie Monster is not a letter," he says indignantly, until at the end of her recitation he humpfs off. The little girl, extremely natural on camera, and obviously not working from a script, looks after him—he's left the screen—and says "I love you." Kermit humpfs back onto the screen and replies, "I love you, too," and then humpfs off again. The responsibility that the adult actors

---

[1] Mark K. Levitan and Susan S. Wieler, "Poverty in New York City, 1969–1999: The Influence of Demographic Change, Income Growth, and Income Inequality," *FRBNY Economic Policy Review* 14, no. 1 (July 2008): 13–30.

and puppeteers feel toward the children, both those with whom they perform and those at home watching—even, it feels like, those watching 45 years later—is plain.

A modern mother might be forgiven for holding down the nearest child as a proxy and decontaminating him.

Another segment opens with a squeal of brakes and a spray of feathers; Big Bird has crossed the street against the light, not at the crosswalk, and has nearly been hit. David takes him to task angrily for being careless and unsafe.

This is a jarring bit—you feel almost as if you have witnessed a meting out of corporal punishment, so unfamiliar is the tone and behavior. Adults on children's shows now do not yell at anyone, and seem to be contractually prevented from it, even in their off-hours. But it's something every parent does at one time or other. Even the nicest parents can be seen flipping out, shouting, spanking, losing their minds, when their child does something actually unsafe.

Seeing an alternative before you, it seems like the respectful distance adults on shows take now only ends up communicating distance. The perfunctory high-fives and "good jobs" do nothing to communicate closeness. *Sesame Street* in 1969 saw itself as *in loco parentis*, and the people on the show acted accordingly. There is loving, correcting, hugging and yelling. A kid can feel cared for by watching it.

An adult watching it is surprised by the extent of the tenderness. My niece, age 12, who had only seen the modern version of the show with disingenuous Elmo and those other painfully disconnected new characters, protested vociferously before watching it with us. After she had seen an old episode, she remarked in surprise: "The new one feels saccharine; this really comes across as earnest."

What has changed in our society that one age's genuine and connected offering to its children now seems completely foreign? The modern Sesame Street organization obviously sees it that way. In the most humiliating and preposterous example of covering one's ass since the admonition to teachers in the public school system never (never!) to touch their students For Any Reason, they have included the warning "not suitable for today's preschoolers" in their reissued DVDs. But what causes this fear? Who are today's children that, like a hornet's nest in a field, we should stay back, and only venture nearby to apply their educational treatment from the other end of a long, sturdy stick?

We have shifted our focus when it comes to poor urban children. Centermost in our minds does not seem to be their education, their safety, their happiness. We are worried over their heft, however. We talk and hear about it constantly. It is a source of constant discussion in the media: We pulled the plug on the cake they got at lunch, we repudiated their chocolate milk. All because we were shocked at their lack of self-control. We noted with horror and surprise: If we offer it, they seem to choose it!

We are not worried enough to give them the hour of gym plus period of recess everyday that they need, nor are we worried enough to fund YMCAs or Boys and Girls Clubs, or to support parks and playgrounds in poor neighborhoods.

We may install beautiful new equipment in well-to-do neighborhoods, but my own informal polling has shown that the equipment is not good at all in the playgrounds frequented by anyone else. Take a trip to the playground in Union Square, with its swinging cattails, ear trumpets, and sweet

What has changed in our society that one age's genuine and connected children's offering now seems completely foreign?

young man who has been hired to put out crayons and help children play catch. Or take a trip to the park at Pier Six or Dumbo.

In contrast, there are the safe but utterly uninspiring walkways that count as playgrounds everywhere else. Sometimes they are grudgingly accented with a little wheel, as if that will make up for the fact that there is nothing actually to climb. These playgrounds are rarely supplied with anything beyond baby swings, just to make it clear to older kids that anyone past four has no cause to be on them at all.

Other than our disturbance over poor children's weight, and that, as I've just pointed out, is given judgmental and hectoring lip service, we let them founder. We focus only on a physically obvious symptom, rather than the disease they and many others in the population suffer from, that is, poverty and despair.

It seems sometimes that we really have resolved to ignore poor children altogether. On television shows, race has become a ubiquity; a great stride forward, of course, but class has dropped out of the discussion entirely. On *Dora the Explorer*, a Latina protagonist gambols through adventures, but she and her cousin Diego live in a purely idealized environment, one which in no way addresses the lives of the 6.1 million Latino kids, more than any other racial or ethnic group, who live in poverty in this country as of 2012.[2] In Dora's life there are no real problems, no ugliness, no small apartments shared with extended family, no threats from immigration, no struggle.

The same can be said for *Ni Hao Kai Lin*, a show starring a little Chinese girl. The only purpose of this show seems to be teaching school children around the country that "ni hao" means "hello" in Chinese. I've watched it once or twice, and it seems they never progress past this initial language lesson. Yet children in Sunset Park and Manhattan's Chinatown would tell you stories about their lives that are inextricably linked with their parents' straitened finances. It's the rare immigrant who begins life on new soil flush and full of opportunity.

The Backyardigans, for all its nicely integrated cast of multiracial animals and catchy songs, represents a suburb of homey perfection. The message is clear: Our society is willing to accept and offer up representations of non-white children, but only if they do not embarrass us with needs, or, by their presence, shame us into rueing our inaction. The personal failure of those who have not made money is a shame that ought not, for politeness's sake, be mentioned.

Just as gentrification has pushed non-affluent New Yorkers to the margins of the city, ending the days when rich and poor lived in the same neighborhoods and were forced to interact, the media has followed suit, committing what is referred to as *symbolic annihilation*. This is to say, in the complete absence of media representation, the lives of poor children, for all intents and purposes, cease to be.

Even *Sesame Street*, the show that helped to create one shared world for kids both rich and poor, the trailblazer on these matters, has dropped the ball. Though the company continues to do an enormous amount of good in the world, and clearly still cares about the meaning behind their original mission, the show itself, their "flagship property," has gone through a transformation. There is a stark difference in tone between then and now.

The difference in tone: Between people and puppets there is an astounding inauthenticity now. Any

[2]Mark Hugo Lopez and Gabriel Velasco, "Childhood Poverty Among Hispanics Sets Record, Leads Nation," (Washington, DC: Pew Research Center, 2011).

interactions with the odious Abby Cadabby prove that. Clearly she has been dreamed up by marketing executives who like to install fairy princesses, their loyal sentinels, in the imaginations of girls to monitor their comings and goings.

The appearance of the set is unrecognizable, as well. From its old incarnation, the street has morphed into affluence, sporting window boxes filled with flowers, and no visible garbage cans. Whether or not they have been doing so in the shitty neighborhoods of New York, someone has been sweeping here.

In New York City, a shocking 30% of children are poor; 30% of NYC families with kids received SNAP benefits,[3] what used to be called food stamps. There are an astounding 21,279 homeless children, and 43% of the residents in public housing are families with children.[4]

Somehow in the almost 45 years since *Sesame Street* debuted, we have developed a prudish aversion to depicting the real conditions of children's lives. The lives of poor children haven't changed though. The least we can give them is to admit that. ❧

---

[3] Ralph da Costa Nunez, Josef Kannegaard and Anne Clark, "The Impact of Food Stamp Benefits on Family Homelessness in New York City," (New York: Institute for Children, Poverty and Homelessness, 2012).

[4] According to the website of the US Department of Housing and Urban Development, accessed August 7, 2013.

IT TAKES 5 SECONDS

Like many of us, you've decided to find a cadre and get to work. But, like many of us, you don't know how to begin. You've gotten off to a lot of false starts, chatting up many likely revolutionists, only to find yourself no better for your efforts. Somehow, when things seem finally to be getting off the ground, some serious disagreement arises, and you wonder to yourself whether x collaborator was really a good fit in the first place.

The Brain Fever Editorial Board is here to solve your problem! It's simple, actually. Real compatibility comes when co-revolutionists like and respect each other. They must have shared values and end goals. Without these, the rest is impossible.

Cut out the following questionnaire, answer this series of one hundred True / False questions yourself, and fold the questionnaire neatly in your wallet. When you run into someone who seems like a potential cadre member, ask them to answer the questions. This should help you to judge compatibility with any fellow travelers you may encounter. If you reach over fifty percent compatibility with this person, you have likely found a new cadre member! ҩ

Answer the following questions true or false:

1	Men and women are guided by hormones, and, in consequence, have different brain chemistry.	T	F
2	Men and women are two different types of human being.	T	F
3	The idea of gender is reductive.	T	F
	If you answered true: Gender is a hoax.	T	F
	If you answered false: In the dark, with no lights on at all, I am aware of my own gender identity.	T	F
4	The Earth Liberation Front is right on the money.	T	F
	If you answered false: There is no emergency. We have at least ten years to deal with climate change.	T	F
5	I eat meat.	T	F
	If you answered yes: But only reclaimed meat.	T	F
6	I believe in zoos.	T	F
7	Inky the Octopus is a folk hero.[1]	T	F
8	Charles Manson is a folk hero.	T	F
9	Guy Debord and Abbie Hoffmann killed themselves because of brain chemistry.	T	F
10	I like television.	T	F
11	The spectacle is not necessarily a negative thing.	T	F

---

[1] Inky the Octopus escaped from the New Zealand National Aquarium and into a nearby bay through a small hole at the top of his tank, never to be recaptured.

12	I enjoy living by proxy.	T	F
13	I shop a lot.	T	F
14	I only shop at Salvation Army.	T	F
15	I would shop secondhand more, but I'm worried about bed bugs.	T	F
16	I make my own clothes.	T	F
17	I knit, but poorly.	T	F
18	I'm uncomfortable around other races.	T	F
19	I have an extreme and salacious interest in other races.	T	F
20	I'm vegan, but I eat cheese.	T	F
21	Communist China jailed my father.	T	F
22	I respect what they were trying to do, but they did it poorly.	T	F
23	I'm still angry about the Jewish Autonomous Oblast.	T	F
24	I was present at Tiananmen Square.	T	F
25	I was present at Woodstock.	T	F
26	I was present in Paris, May 1968.	T	F
27	I was present at the WTO protests in Seattle.	T	F
28	I was present at Occupy Oakland.	T	F

29	After retirement, I see myself living on the street.	T	F
30	After retirement, I see myself living in an ecovillage, leading life-cycle rituals as resident crone.	T	F
31	After retirement, I see myself living on a boat because my city of birth is flooded.	T	F
32	I would like to live off the grid.	T	F
33	I would like to be the one to short out the grid.	T	F
34	I tell people I would like to live off the grid, but I really like Facebook.	T	F
35	Zuckerberg will be the first one with his head on a pike.	T	F
36	I believe our modern digital connectivity has led to positive interactions between people.	T	F
37	I consider myself a digital organizer.	T	F
38	The Internet hasn't mattered for anti-establishment types since The Well.	T	F
39	Fuck the Internet.	T	F
40	I watched *Star Trek* as a kid, and it gave me a vision of the future.	T	F
41	I watched *Star Trek* as a kid, and it traumatized me.	T	F
42	Like Jesus, Sly Stone is too beautiful for this world.	T	F
43	My parents were in the Living Theater.	T	F

44	I was in the Living Theater.	T	F
45	I got the clap from a member of the Living Theater.	T	F
46	I believe in free love.	T	F
47	I believe the Weathermen were right to eschew cigarettes.	T	F
48	The only revolution that matters is a cultural revolution.	T	F
49	The only revolution that matters is a workers' revolution.	T	F
50	As someone raised in the Bourgeoisie, I genuinely fear what would happen if the workers rose up.	T	F
51	The only revolution that matters is one centered on race.	T	F
52	The only revolution that matters is a women's revolution.	T	F
53	The only revolution that matters is a queer revolution.	T	F
54	I don't use the term queer anymore.	T	F
55	I consider myself queer, but only sexually.	T	F
56	I consider myself queer, but only my personality.	T	F
57	I am queer both sexually and in terms of my personality.	T	F

58	The first step to the revolution is leafleting.	T	F
59	The first step to the revolution is zines.	T	F
60	The first step to the revolution is marches and civil disobedience.	T	F
61	The first step to the revolution is breaking windows.	T	F
62	The best outcome of revolutionary action is a barter economy.	T	F
63	The best outcome of revolutionary action is bankers forced to clean toilets.	T	F
64	The best outcome of revolutionary action is a network of anticapitalist nodes.	T	F
65	I'd like to live in one, but I'm afraid of who else might be there.	T	F
66	I don't like backrubs.	T	F
67	I am allergic to cats.	T	F
68	I own a copy of the *Moosewood Cookbook*, but I haven't used it since college.	T	F
69	I consider myself urban, but I'm not black.	T	F
70	I'm black and rural.	T	F
71	I resent the American narrative of race as binary.	T	F
72	The last person on Earth will be Chinese.	T	F

73	My grandparents were Communists.	T	F
74	My grandparents were Socialists.	T	F
75	My grandparents were Anarchists.	T	F
76	As a teenager, I had carnal knowledge of Allen Ginsburg.	T	F
77	As a teenager, I had carnal knowledge of Stokely Carmichael.	T	F
78	As a teenager, I had carnal knowledge of Alger Hiss.	T	F
79	I don't mind going to jail.	T	F
80	I've been to jail already several times.	T	F
81	I'm a fast runner.	T	F
82	I'm a good writer.	T	F
83	I'm fearless.	T	F
84	I'm timid.	T	F
85	I'm already entangled in the status quo.	T	F
86	I have no skin in the game.	T	F
87	I own property.	T	F
88	I own a printing press.	T	F
89	I'm tired of atomization.	T	F
90	I don't care what happens as long as it isn't this.	T	F

91	I never pursued a career because I was waiting for society to end.	T	F
92	I worry about what would happen to the libraries in the event of a real revolution.	T	F
93	I can live without dental care.	T	F
94	I like the idea of democracy, but I'd like to have more to do.	T	F
95	I'm a Maoist.	T	F
96	I'm a Trotskyite.	T	F
97	I'm a Situationist.	T	F
98	I'm a Liberation Theologist.	T	F
99	I'm a Catholic Worker.	T	F
100	I'm free on Thursdays.	T	F

Support Your Local Library!

Where else can you find fairly clean public bathrooms, beleagured but resilient public servants, and rooms and rooms filled with books, all available for you to take out and enjoy?

Distract yourself from your troubles!

Do better on your GREs!

Learn to make lutefisk!

The public library is the heart of the republic!

Avail Yourself!

YOU'RE FROM DIGITARIA.

YES.

I GREW UP THERE. I CAME HERE TO CORONISPORT WHEN I WAS NINETEEN YEARS OLD.

BUT YOU **LEARNED** HOW TO PLAY IN **SAGALA**

THAT'S RIGHT.

WHAT WAS IT LIKE THERE WHEN YOU WERE GROWING UP?

OH, IT'S A WONDERFUL PLACE TO BE A YOUNG BOY.

IT'S WARM AND **GREEN**, THE AIR IS FRESH, AND THE **FOOD** IS THE BEST IN THE GALAXY.

NOW I KNOW YOU SPENT A LOT OF TIME **PRACTICING**.

BUT WHAT KIND OF **TROUBLE** DID YOU GET INTO?

I WOULD HAVE TO SAY ALL KINDS OF TROUBLE.

FOR EXAMPLE?

IT'S BEEN THIRTY YEARS NOW.

YES. I'VE BEEN PLAYING THERE FOR THIRTY YEARS.

YET YOU STILL HAVE A PASSION FOR IT.

OH, YES.

I NEED TO PLAY. IT DOESN'T MUCH MATTER WHERE.

ANYWAY, I RETIRED FROM THE ORCHESTRA.

I ONLY PLAY JAZZ ON MONDAYS AND TUESDAYS, WHICH CAN GET REALLY EXPERIMENTAL.

AND I DO THE SHOW, OF COURSE.

BUT YOU SEEM TO BE PERFORMING MORE THAN EVER OUTSIDE THE CLUB.

SINCE LEAVING THE ORCHESTRA, YES.

I'VE ENJOYED TEAMING UP WITH LOTS OF DIFFERENT PEOPLE.

ALTHOUGH THERE IS ONE CONSTANT: THE SAXOPHONE OF GERARD "GILLY" DEMBELE.

YES, WE EVEN GREW UP TOGETHER, BACK IN SAGALA.

I HAVE A PHOTOGRAPH THAT I'D LIKE TO SHOW.

OKAY.

SEVEN AND A HALF LIGHT-YEARS IN THIS CASE, ALL THE WAY TO THE REMOTE COLONY OF HIGHTOWER.

THE COLONY WAS IN THE MIDST OF A YEARS-LONG BATTLE WITH A LEGITIMATE PLAGUE THAT THEY HAVE YET TO ERADICATE COMPLETELY.

WHAT HAPPENED WHEN THIS RECORDING ARRIVED THERE?

I AM TOLD THAT THE SIMULCAST OF THE FIRST LIVE CONCERT BROUGHT CATHARSIS.

SALES, TOO.

OH YES. ONE STEP CLOSER TO THE BEACH!

YOU'VE BEEN INVITED TO PERFORM THERE.

NOT ME! THINGS MOVE FAST ENOUGH FOR ME AS THEY ARE.

I'D LIKE TO SEE THE WORLD IN FIFTEEN YEARS, BUT IN FIFTEEN YEARS, YOU KNOW WHAT I MEAN?

IN THE MEANTIME, YOU SEEM TO BE BOOKED SOLID.

INDEED.

IN ADDITION TO THE RE-RELEASE OF **HALF-FULL**, YOUR LATEST ALBUM WITH THE ENSEMBLE **TRANSGENESIS** IS CALLED **DOMICILE**, DUE OUT NOVEMBER THE EIGHTH.

IF YOU'RE IN THE AREA, HOWEVER, TREAT YOURSELF TO A LIVE PERFORMANCE.

CELEBRATE **HALLOWEEN** WITH TRANSGENESIS AT THE FRANKS OPERA HOUSE.

ON FRIDAY, NOVEMBER FOURTH, MISTER LOULY WILL APPEAR AT THE WROBEL AUDITORIUM WITH LAUREN PEÑA, MISTER DEMBÉLÉ, AND NELSON "PENGO" PAGAN.

YOU CAN ALSO CATCH HIM MONDAYS AND TUESDAYS AT EVE'S TEMPTATION, AND EVERY WEEKNIGHT ON AUMEA PRIME.

CHECK YOUR LOCAL LISTINGS FOR DETAILS.

MISTER LOULY, THANK YOU **SO** MUCH FOR JOINING US.

MY PLEASURE.

clap! clap! clap! clap! clap! clap! clap!

AND THANK **YOU** FOR TUNING IN.

GOOD NIGHT!

clap! clap! clap! clap! clap! clap!

Now available for your leisure-time enjoyment, a Science fiction Story replete with over 50 high-quality pen and ink illustrations:

HOMESICK for EARTH by OLIVIA SCHANZER

Read this first installment in the adventures of Vera Mironova, a Russian girl who travels to the planet Sobek with her parents, crack translators for the United planets with imperfectly Suppressed nervous Conditions.

Join her as she attempts to acclimate to life among upright lizard people who enjoy self-governance and horticulture, and commute to work on ornery animals who will not tolerate prodding. Suitable for those who can read and those who never bothered, the very young, the wide Swath in the middle, and those in their early and late dotage.

And available at Amazon in book and ebook form.

To Land a Man

*A Novel
by Olivia Schanzer*

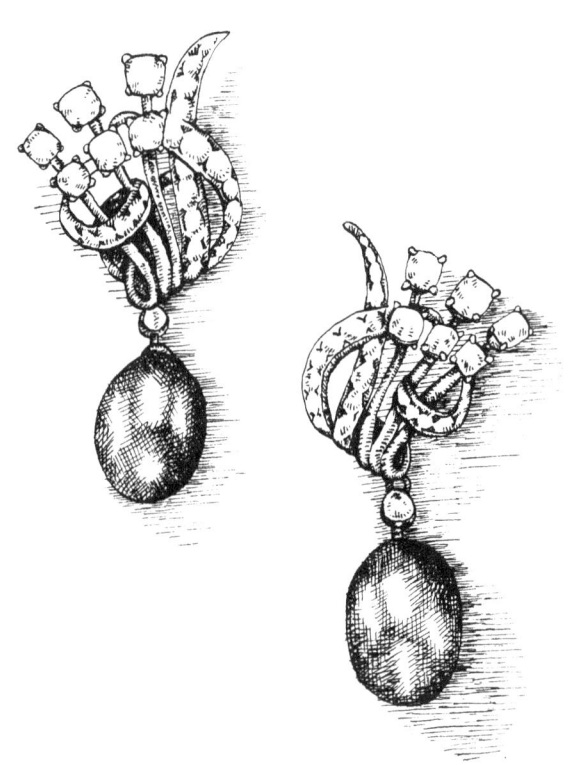

I

In truth, this was Mrs Wallace's last effort on her daughter's behalf. She had tried and tried to no avail. She had tried over and above what good people would have done, and it was now, officially, a waste of her time. Good people could only do so much, especially if their offspring were unwilling to be helped. No man to speak of, and no marriage, and Katherine was fast approaching thirty, although Mrs Wallace reminded Katherine not to mention that. Quite often in social situations, Katherine mentioned it; so often, in fact, that it seemed as if she were going out of her way to rankle: "Well, my friends and I are all approaching thirty. . . ." At her mother's parties, propped up against the wainscoting and holding forth, she introduced every thought with this, linked ideas and sentences with these strange words, even when there was no visible link. How had the protocol changed so much since they were young? Mrs Wallace and her friends could not understand. In nature, as in civilization, this truth was steadfast: an aging mate was no pretty thing. Therefore, who would reference such a fact?

The only consolation to Mrs Wallace was how many of her friends were in the same predicament. It seemed that none of this generation wanted to grow into adulthood. Did they wish to remain forever propped up against their mothers' wainscoting? Or was it that they could not grow up? Mrs Wallace wondered if they had somehow produced an entire generation of rejects, girls who ought to be thrown back on the scrap pile. What were they doing wrong? Her friends' daughters were generally pretty, they had gone to college, they had interesting things to talk about—though they did not take them out as often as they might—but there was something not quite right about them that, Mrs Wallace imagined, made them unattractive to creditable men.

Some of them had been in long-term relationships. Katherine, for instance. Katherine had been seeing a graduate student named Doug for a number of years. The name puckered Mrs Wallace's lips. He was not able to finish his dissertation, seemed no longer to be working on it, in fact, and had spent, for all Mrs Wallace could see, the last few years fluttering on the edge of academia with no termination point in sight. Obviously, he was not the man Mrs Wallace would have picked out for her daughter. When asked if she liked him, Mrs Wallace often left it at these simple words and brooked no quarter for the person who continued to pry. But for the most part, Mrs Wallace denied that he existed at all, and his appearance at events was always a surprise to those of her acquaintances who had heard her speak of her daughter.

To deny him was not fully possible, of course. The fact of him was insistent, for he kept popping up when Katherine was invited anywhere. One might be very sad about it if one's hope for the human race had not yet run out, as in all his infirmity, he did not stick out as much as he should have; he was of a kind with all the other escorts brought around. Even her mother's other daughter, Mrs Chester, who would not admit that she had, had created several such as these. She had made three nephews for Mrs Wallace whom she was not proud to claim.

Perhaps this was the caliber of men available to them. Tall and short, lovely girls with good hair and good complexions, ended up with ciphers. Stale, plain men, without much money, without much charisma, spunk, manliness. By looks alone, these girls had earned much more on any market she understood, but then, the value of the currency seemed to have changed since she was young.

Her best friend, Larinda, who lived in an apartment building several blocks over from her own, in the seventies by the park, had a daughter who just this previous June had married such a man. About this wedding Larinda cooed and swooned in public, but her private emotions were very different. She had thrown a colossal wedding with bone china and a string quartet and the *New York Times* photographer snapping, snapping away. Larinda, in her good jewels and a dress so stylish, so much more than the mother of the bride, had held court, and done so radiantly. In all its trappings, the union had really seemed something for which to be thankful, and Larinda had done such a good job making it so. There were not many who could ascertain Larinda's additional feelings.

Mrs Wallace, who herself may have had additional feelings, put them aside when the wedding photos returned from the photographer's studio, thematically arranged in their large leather albums, and sat, in fulfillment of her role, lingering over them with her friend. The pictures were very artful and sophisticated—that was how the photographer described them when asked to defend the close-up of the bridesmaid weeping piteously in the bathroom—and there were a certain number in black and white to capture the experience timelessly. It was not due to dumb luck, but because Larinda had very good taste, and knew the difference when selecting a photographer. She had not succumbed to her daughter's strange request that they hire a man she knew to do the whole thing electronically. To this Larinda had replied, and made Mrs Wallace proud in her recapitulation, "Perhaps you would like to do it yourself with an Instamatic, Dahlia." Yet as they sat together looking over them, one thing was remarkably clear to them both, and no amount of fair lighting or thoughtful use of focus could conceal it—for the fact of it pressed them deeper into the pink silk cushions of Larinda's dressing room sofa (the albums were extremely heavy and took two laps to bear their weight)—how far beneath her Dahlia had married.

After all, here was Dahlia, posed with several lilies against the backdrop of the bridge, as tall as was proper, slim and swathed in the most rapturous silk gown, with smooth, light hair and eyes illuminated by the clear afternoon sun, an aquiline nose, a beatific smile on her face, and here was her husband, who seemed to have pulled shadows out of the sky just for himself. It seemed he was working actively to remain unattractive against adversaries that fought to flatter him: his own good looks, his wife, her flowers, and the elegant line of the bridge. He had a terrible way of carrying himself, and it was here epitomized. Too, he was full of the weasel, oily, arrogant, and for what? What had he to be so arrogant about? Even a casual observer must ask. But all Larinda could do was sigh, and turn her friend's attention to the subject of the gold photo edges once again—they seemed of exceptionally good quality—and allow Mrs Wallace to gather the rest; Larinda could hardly even utter the name of Dahlia's husband, whose intrusion had ruined so many of the wedding pictures.

"At least that daughter of yours has been married off," Mrs Wallace told Larinda as they sat with the stately albums between them on their laps, although she had not been asked for advice, not with words. Larinda sat with an unconscious hand resting loosely over a picture of Dahlia's husband, blocking him out. Mrs Wallace could see, between Larinda's fingers, that he was helping a flower girl jump over a puddle, and smiling sincerely. "At least you will not have to spend your elder years in a constant state of dismay, worrying about her. You need not worry who will take care of her when you are gone, and she is old, and she has no husband at all, and is pensioned off from her dingy job after a life of childless work. At least these things need no longer concern you."

Larinda merely sighed again. "Oh," she exhaled, "I appreciate your kind words, but you mustn't pretend for my sake. You must not candy-coat it for me," and accepted Mrs Wallace's gentle patting.

About her own maternal distress, Mrs Wallace cried out on the telephone to Larinda quite often. "I pray he never asks her to marry him. I could not stand for him to be my relative."

But Larinda, who always tried to be encouraging, even when consumed by her own despair—and remembered Mrs Wallace's own words—would say back to her, "Would you prefer Katherine as an old maid?" It was no consolation to Mrs Wallace; she had only brought that up to make Larinda feel better.

Doug was everything Mrs Wallace did not like in a man. Though she had no photographs of him to stare at in dismay, she had seen the real version enough to know. He was, as Dahlia's husband was, a little oily, but to this he added ineffectuality, a plague of mildewed skin, and the seeming inability to earn one penny over the minimum wage. He could not do the things for Katherine that must be done; neither would he do for Katherine what only should be done. And, Mrs Wallace suspected, it was not just because he did not have the money to do so, though, of course, it was not presently in his pocket. Mrs Wallace was in fact quite sure that there was some in the family, waiting for the day when he reached some amorphous majority that had nothing to do with age, and ceased to be this boy with graying hair he played so avidly. This, Mrs Wallace reasoned, had to be the case, since who could be so relentlessly unambitious if he had nothing to fall back on?

Nevertheless, whether there was or was not money waiting for him,

Doug made no moves in the direction of manhood. The way he acted made it seem as if he had not received one moment of training, and was primed, most resolutely, to go nowhere at all. Here was that type of good-for-nothing who did not even give his seat up for old women on the subway, or help old men with heavy doors. Here was a man who had no manners. He typed while he talked on the phone, and talked loudly on the phone while he rode on the bus; he did not remember his mother's birthday. And yet he had gone to good schools, where, Mrs Wallace remembered from her youth, they used to punish boys without manners, and teach swimming as well. There was no reason for him to carry himself so badly.

It was not so much that she had evidence of these particular breaches; it was just that she suspected. Katherine had brought him over for dinner at least ten times in the past five years, and Mrs Wallace had talked to him and asked him questions, although she had not been particularly keen on hearing the answers. These long talks reaped nothing about his personality that pinned him, definitively, in the camp of rudeness. There was something rude about him, but it was in his whole being, not in any one action. Still, Mrs Wallace suspected him, and she had a long track record of being correct about these things. When she went to a wedding, she usually made a note in her leather date book as to whether the groom would leave the wife later on in their marriage, and she was usually correct about it when she checked back. It might not happen right away, but it was sure to happen one day. There was something ineffably present in a doomed relationship, just as there was something ineffably present, a kinetic energy, in Doug, that made her know he was rude.

Perhaps Doug was shifty, and tried to hide it, Mrs Wallace told her husband. And really, he seemed a little slow-witted, focused on the intellectual side of life, but with none of the real insight. Of course it was clear that he was too weak and thin to have pursued a career that required manliness, and perhaps this had been a sort of default choice. He had not the nerve for business, nor the charm for politics, and neither did he do well with other people, which most of the remaining jobs required. He always drank too little when he came to dinner, and made the other guests feel uncomfortable, as if he were watching them. All of these things could not help but keep him out of most of the rewarding careers. And then there was the problem that he was not at all impressed by anything that they had to offer, and didn't seem to be much interested either, which was plainly bad manners, although of a more subtle kind. "Do you like the food?" she would be made to ask, and he would reply reluctantly, "Yes." "What do you think of this book I'm reading?" Mr Wallace would ask, and he would nod his head and very quickly say, "I've heard of it." All that they did he rebuffed. Perhaps an individual whom one encountered briefly might tolerate this level of neglect, but she had never heard of an instance when a man for whom one worked would. This was as true for surgeons as it was for stock analysts.

When Mrs Wallace asked Doug about his dissertation, cursorily and without a hint of interest present in her face or her voice, he looked askance at her, as if he were a woman whose doctor had just asked her weight. "If you're interested, I could give you a copy of the first chapter." The first chapter had never materialized when it was asked after, however, and Mrs Wallace felt sure that there was no first chapter at all.

Many nights Mrs Wallace broke the silence in her sitting room to speak on the issue of Doug. The sitting room was where she and Mr Wallace sat to read in the evening when they stayed in, and where Mr Wallace kept his personal chair, from which the old horsehair stuffing was always reasserting itself, and needing to be stuffed back in with a firm hand and a professional's tools every few years.

Mr Wallace, from the comfort of this chair, would not acknowledge these flaws in Doug, as he could not read nuance capably; it was his personal platform that she should just hope for Katherine's happiness, and leave it at that.

"And what may I hope for if I leave it alone?" she would demand of him. "What sort of happiness can I expect? A happiness for her that is in direct opposition to my own? Is that all you would wish for me?"

Mr Wallace would look back down at what he was reading and try to ignore her. He was an imperfect ignorer, however, and Mrs Wallace could always see that, breaking the only rule of the task, he looked up from time to time in her direction.

The girls! Lord knew what they were going to do with the girls. Here, Mrs Wallace saw, was a generation of young women who would have to carry their men around like sacks of potatoes. There would be no good earner in the family, and the women, financially responsible as they were doomed to be, would be forced to look after one more dependent. Mrs Wallace had little confidence in Katherine's ability to do that. Mr and Mrs Wallace could not be expected to support her in perpetuity. They must care for their own financial needs. When one had a child, was one expected to maintain them in a childlike state for the whole of their life? Was this a permanent commitment? She could not believe it was so, and yet so many of these children required constant financial intervention.

"When I was a girl and you a young man," Mrs Wallace might begin, "the boys would pick up the whole cost of the date, and they did not take girls out if they couldn't afford to treat them. Do you remember the little silver purse for mad money that I would wear around my neck? The one that was my aunt's? How much do you really think that held?" It had held a dime or two and nothing larger, kept only in the event that she needed to call home. When she was dating, she had been much younger than Katherine. It wasn't that long ago that all these things had been standard, and not at all peculiar to herself.

"How much did it hold?" Mr Wallace said with only slight attention, for in the evening he went back to his newspapers for a second look, and finished any article for which he had not had the time during the day. "Mrs Wallace, you would think that the man was homeless. He is a student; he's not an indigent! Manners have changed. Men are no longer required to pay for every incidental when they take a girl out. Though we never told you, that was always a terrible strain on our wallets. I would have to eat hot dogs for dinner three days straight after a date with you. I hope it's not the case that you don't like him only because he doesn't have money." This was the insult, though stated mildly, less declarative and more questioning, that her husband believed was his most trenchant. For several years in college, he had been a great friend to the lumpen proletariat, she remembered, and had never since been able fully to sever this allegiance.

"Of course, that's not why you don't like him," Larinda had said to her later, for Mrs Wallace had absented herself from Mr Wallace in order to call Larinda from the bedroom; she wished to make her point clear to somebody who was receptive to it, and had not the time nor energy to help Mr Wallace to see. "Dahlia's husband just got a new job, and he's making loads of money, yet he will be a blind spot on those pictures. I am thinking of scrubbing him out with a little lye."

"At least she's married," Mrs Wallace began her refrain, for they each had their own, and this was Mrs Wallace's. "At least she is accounted for. But Katherine is caught between two worlds, neither of them attractive. I shiver at her future as much as at her present, Larinda. For one does not long to imagine their daughter a middle-aged woman on dates, does one? A mother is supposed to protect her child from indignity and deprivation. But this child will not agree to it. It seems she cannot even see she is at risk."

"It's not just Katherine, Mrs Wallace. The whole generation has been blinded. You have told me that yourself: 'None of them can do what for us was so easy.' You said that very thing. 'It's not so much to ask to make a reasonable marriage, and a life to go along with it. Yet none of them can seem to.'" Mrs Wallace nodded, though really she had not called to listen to Larinda. It was no consolation that others had failed as well; she and Larinda had both failed their children. No matter what had caused it, no matter how universal a problem it was, Larinda could not clothe it in solidarity and thereby make it presentable; it was a profoundly unattractive thing. ❧

SUBWAY SKETCHBOOK

by Agir

WHY WE OCCUPY

LIBERTY PLAZA 2011

INTERVIEWS BY OLIVIA SCHANZER

In 2011, in a free display of their constitutional right to assembly, people across America, and in countries around the world, occupied public space. Though they were a heterogeneous group, all displayed a general dissatisfaction with the radical inequality of our country. All displayed the opinion that America had run afoul of its founding purpose. Five years later, we can hardly say this feeling has left us. The vitriol of the present election surely is the dark side of what was the buoyancy of the Occupy movement.

As a means to draw attention to a cause, the tactic of occupation is unimpeachable. The Standing Rock Sioux in North Dakota are at present occupying space to protest a pipeline scheduled to be built under the Missouri River, upstream and within hailing distance of their reservation. They have been encamped in small numbers since early spring of this year, and beginning in July, when work began in earnest, they have swelled their numbers to around three thousand, with Native allies and others from around the country joining them. They have plans to stay encamped somehow through the frigid Midwestern winter.

The following interview is excerpted from the book *Why We Occupy*, a collection of interviews taken in Liberty Plaza in downtown Manhattan during the Occupy Wall Street. Why did the people occupy? What were their purposes and goals? Of course, they will have to answer that themselves. ℯ

Cynthia

When you spend the day here, you really understand the workings of it. The biggest misconception is that there's no organization, no leaders. Me and my friend Eric just came back from our coordinators' meeting at nine, and we were saying that in our opinion, the organization is sort of centralized/decentralized. That means there's tons of information, not that there's no goal. The goal is, essentially, equality in this abundant world. It is centralized here in the park, but with so many different concerns to that goal.

It's not just specific to New York or America; it's the abundance of the world. It's also a way back to the spirit and soul of humanity, meaning equality, human dignity, fairness, democracy, voices being heard. It's those voices that may have been on the fringes, that were not about to be heard. And it's not just race, because it's white, Mexican, African American ... it's everything. Also, there's a class that hasn't been as educated that we're trying to include and allow a voice to.

We have our General Assembly every day at seven. We also have our working group meetings and our occupiers' meetings. Many people are intimidated by the word "meeting" because they don't know how to voice themselves. They're afraid they're not going to learn properly how to be heard, or they get frustrated because they're not being heard. So they hear "meetings" and they want to stay away. That's what I mean: It's decentralized because we want to include everybody's voices. We are really working hard to do that.

Today I work at Info/Outreach. I've been here thirty-three days. I'm living here. I've worked in our Comfort, our kitchen, and our Sanitation. My thing is outreaching to communities—not just passer-bys and tourists, but also our communities here within the park.

Being here in Zuccotti Park is an important stance. It's not a fight; it's a stance. It says that we are here. We're not leaving until we get some changes within our socio-political-economic system.

Our current systems, since before the economic meltdown in 2008, have been not working. So we voted with President Obama. His whole platform was changes, and we feel that we haven't gotten the changes from his presidency. We gave that opportunity. He said, "Changes are coming. Changes are coming." These changes have been an issue for many, many years in our socio-political-economic system. People put their hope in Obama's changes. We thought it was a new era. I personally believe that he did try through struggles, but it hasn't happened.

Since the changes haven't arrived yet, I think, collectively, something happened with us as humanity, as a people, as all peoples. We've been waiting. We've been waiting. We've been waiting. They pushed it back to another agenda, pushed it back to the next agenda and the next agenda. And now, for some reason, you can just witness—what is it?—fifty countries all over the world now standing up for humanity, for dignity, for equality.

It's a universal upwelling.

It *is* an upwelling. My point is: It's been a long time coming, and the most beautiful thing that happened was that collectively, the peoples of the world are standing together. That's not happened in our country since the civil rights movement, where they said, "This undignified behavior is not working for humanity." So this is the special thing about it: collectively, everybody standing together.

This outreach that happens within the park—how does that work?

There are several of us who realize the importance of reaching out within our community. We are trying to reach out to people not just from working groups. We are all about compassionate, dignified equality for *all* peoples. Not all peoples who gather here know how to make the changes happen, but they want to be involved.

People are drawn here because they feel protected. They don't really know how to fit in, but they're drawn here. It may not seem like it. It may seem like they're just here hanging out, but it's because they're not included yet. They're intimidated to come to our meetings, our working groups. This was a big discussion today.

It's not just about race; it's not just about people of color, or Latin people, white, black, whatever. It's a certain type of people who have been on the fringes of society. They've just been on the wrong side of our society. They have been, maybe, outcast because they've been institutionalized, either mentally or for addiction to drugs or alcohol. They've been let out of the prisons or mental institutions, and they're thrown into these homeless shelters.

In essence, political leaders like our mayor and so forth of this city are saying, "You have somewhere to go. You have a homeless shelter. We provide you this." Well, those are more dangerous than prisons. People don't want to go there; that's why we have homelessness.

But the one percent—for instance, our Mayor Bloomberg ... what he said the other day, that we defeat our presence here because of all the homelessness, all the drugs? Those happen in the streets whether Occupy Wall Street's here or not. That's been ongoing. I mean, it's silly. Does he think he's the mayor of Walt Disney World? This is New York City, one of the toughest cities in the world. These things have gone on and will go on whether Occupy Wall Street's here or not, but because we were getting these people here—homeless and runaway kids and drug addicts and alcoholics . . .

I take it upon myself to go into these areas within our camp. People are not aware of how facilitation works in our meetings, so we're inviting them to come to a Facilitation Working Group meeting. You can facilitate in meetings, or just be a part—a voice. Or at least, just have an awareness of what you choose. You can actively be in our meeting. You are invited. You are welcome.

So there's small pockets of us who are initiating that on our own, as individuals. We're getting together and making a nice introduction and report with many people here within the camp, not just here where it's nice and clean, at the library or in Info/Outreach—see, this is pretty—but all throughout the camp, wherever we can include people.

We say, "Hi, I'm Cynthia. I work in Info. Do you know about the meeting today? It's going to be at four o'clock." A lot of people here in our park, like in society, do not have access to computers or fancy iPods or cell phones or smart phones. You can't just give them a flyer, or say, "Go to N-Y-C-G-A dot net." Chances are, they won't read it. They may not have the capacity to connect with it because they feel like, "Ugh, it's just another paper thrown at me."

So on a human level, that's what I mean about coming back to the spirit and soul of humanity. Olivia, you know, we're interacting as human beings—in the eye—and that's what we do here.

That's what we feel is very important. If we're saying the ninety-nine percent . . . which I feel, personally, is a terrible tag. I feel like here in this park, we are one hundred percent. We are one hundred percent, so I don't really like that victimized ninety-nine percent, myself. That's my personal opinion. I don't really like that. We're saying we're the ninety-nine percent? Well, ninety-nine percent is not just a certain educated class that's doing the meetings. Ninety-nine percent is: Everyone should be included, if you really have that heart.

That's what our coordinators' meeting started to be about. It got a little too much on that subject, because the coordinators' meeting every morning is just report-backs for every working group. It's for any urgent or vital information that's currently going on, but it started to get into that discussion. So it will be a breakout group, which they started discussing after that meeting.

A few of us decided to just go throughout the camp and talk: "Oh, this meeting is about this and that and the other," or, "The way it works is like this," or, "Direct Action is a group of people that works on protests and marches." Telling people these kinds of things—really verbally communicating within our camp—so that we can grow this with the people who showed up here. The stance of the people here is so important, and as you know, the symbolic stance of being here ... if this park goes away, we don't have Occupy Wall Street, so we need to build this up thoroughly. We're doing that. We are working on it.

How are people reacting to the outreach?

I'm saying outreach, but we do—

Inreach.

Right! Yes, exactly! People that I outreach to, and other people ... it's great! It's sort of like, "Okay, thank you." You know, some people are a little hardened, so they won't say thank you, but you can see in the face and in the eyes how they start to soften. It's a beautiful thing, because people don't want to admit that they don't know what's going on. You can see in their face it's one of those a-ha moments. You can see in their face when they're like, "That feels so good!"

At our meeting, we also talked about the vernacular of speech. Everyone has a different vernacular. We have a group here who comes from the streets, and we have a group here who comes from a more educated class. So that's also inreach/outreach that we're doing, to try to connect those two vernaculars so that we can all relate. Some people who are more expressive or more passionate—they're not yelling or being forceful. They're not being angry; they're just talking, and we have to allow that. We have to be open. It's not for us to say, "No! Talk when *we* want you to talk! Have a meeting the way *we* want you to have a meeting! Compose yourself! Don't do this, the way *we* don't do this!" No, no, no, because some people who talk like that can be passive-aggressive, and it's not a good thing. It's actually a real wall.

This really is a beautiful challenge. It's the most beautiful challenge because if we can make this work, we're proving so much about the beauty of humanity.

How do you take what's being learned here and bring it outwards into the bigger world?

We do have an Outreach group. In fact, they have a meeting today. What they do is they have, like, a luncheon, and they invite people from different boroughs to hold their own G.A.'s. They learn how we facilitate G.A.'s. They learn how to gather a stronger voice. And we're spreading this, through the outreach program, to all the boroughs.

You should probably go. It would be interesting for you to see that. Everybody's invited. That way you can actually talk to other people, and that would answer that question, "What would it be outside the occupation?" We all really do want to hear each other, help each other, spread the knowledge and education. We really do want to grow as a society of humanity. That is what's happening. That's what's happening throughout the world now.

In the beginning, we had this wonderful world map, and we put pins on all the places that are being occupied. We have since lost it, although it might be in our S.I.S., because you know, we've had snowstorms, rainstorms, evictions and cleanups, and it's gotten a bit lost. Smithsonian museum representatives have come down to acquire it when our movement is done. That and our map of Zuccotti Park. I love the Smithsonian, and this is really history.

That's why we're making a book, to set down the real history. The press has been pretty skewed—not accurate at all.

Of course, the *Post* and Fox. Bill O'Reilly—who's a cotton-ass—said on his program the other day, "There's going to be murder!" You know, there's a murder on the streets of New York, in all the boroughs, probably more than once every day. But that is a city. That has nothing to do with us being here. We are actually providing a lot more safety to the streets that has never been in this area.

We just had a harm-reduction group coming in. They're making us aware that the people who come here—you know, the addicts and the alcoholics—they need the help. There are areas here that have been able to help them, to assist them, to give them that compassion, and to at least make it safer for them, so they can hopefully get out of that addiction or that phase in their lives. We have our medics here to treat the homeless—our medics, our volunteers, our nurses, our doctors, our psychologists on staff. We have acupuncturists.

For the mayor to say something so ignorant . . . it shows him to be out of touch. He is a part of the one percent that we are actually making a stand against.

Someone described him as "the hammer of the one percent."[1]

[1]Douglas A. Muzzio, in: Kate Taylor, "Demonstrators Test Mayor, a Backer of Wall St. and Free Speech" (*New York Times*, November 3, 2011).

So the harm-reduction people were trying to link you guys into the services they have in the area?

Yes. We have our guy Stephen, at the library, that works with Scales. He is an ex-addict, and he has had a wonderful doctor who helped him through it. Now he's clean. He's wonderful, he's productive, and he's great, so he's trying to help other people. The doctor brought his colleagues and representatives—who were all over the boroughs, like up in the Bronx—to come down here to hand out pamphlets, and to have a meeting with us. They know we have this issue with people being safe: Do they feel safe as they come here?

That's something that the press and media don't like. They just like to say that people are gathering here causing trouble. No, they're gathering here and feeling safe because we have Community Outreach, Community Watch, Nonviolent Communication, safety class, . . .

I've done many night watches from two to four in the morning. Around the coffee, partner up. We go around and we do this in such a way that we make a presence within our community, to prevent any kind of unsavory acts. I love that I just said "unsavory," but you know what I mean. So our presence here, actually, is a very good thing. It's an educating thing. It's a knowledge-is-compassion thing.

The people that are against it—the *Post*, Bill O'Reilly, Fox News, all the other news that are saying these negative things—it's really embarrassing for them as a human. People are getting fed and clothed and a place to sleep. There are a lot of compassionate people here. That's what I meant about the beauty of humanity: There's so many beautiful, compassionate people. The Empathy table is for everyone.

It's really an amazing thing, but you know, at the same time, please understand that this is incredibly, incredibly difficult work. It's very, very hard work. I've been here thirty-three days, not only getting used to sleeping outside because of the noise and the weather and so on and so forth, but actively getting up and doing Community Watch, and thwarting fights and issues like that.

And then just our passions and our emotions. We sometimes fight or we argue, but they're friendly arguments. We make up within our groups. Our passions, our emotions . . . we're like, "Aagh!" because it's very difficult work. Sometimes you feel like you're making so much progress, and then some fool will come and rouse up people and get people to work against, and a lot of them are paid to do this.

Really.

I know that for a fact because someone from our group was sitting at a café, and there's a gentleman here

... everybody knows him. He's a black guy. He has this beard. He comes almost every single day, mouths people off talking about, oh, he's a one-percenter. He spreads these just terrible messages, and someone heard him say—in a café, talking with someone else—that he's paid to be here, to do that.

I worked my first days here in Comfort, and I know for a fact that the guy I helped—he was so sweet—said he just got out of Rikers. He was holding up his pants because they didn't give him his belt back. There's apparently some new system where you have to sign something to get the rest of your things back. I don't know what that was about, but we gave him a belt. Not only gave him a belt, but new jeans, new clothes. We kept him warm, gave him a place to sleep, and he marched with us. We told him as much as we could about what it was about. I can't say I've seen him here again, but I know that these people are coming.

We hear that they're let out of jail and told to come here because it's safe. In Tribeca, there's a homeless man who's been there about twenty years. We know for a fact that the police woke him up, told him to come here. We know that for a fact because he told us that. He actually was a very intelligent man. It was his choice to be homeless, and he wasn't just some crazy rabble rouser, or a harmful man.

So we know in those three instances that, yes, people are told to come here. It is safe here, and we do take care of them. We have the compassion. Can you imagine what a beautiful society this would be if everyone did that?

Every time I come here, I wonder why this can't exist outside.

We're hoping it can. That's what the outreach is about: to get past these borders, to get the word out to the boroughs. And it is being spread out throughout the world now. It's really good! Exciting!

Would you tell me about your background in activism?

I'm not an activist. I've never been an activist. I've never marched a day in my life for nothing. I've been in New York over fifteen years. I do hair and makeup for film and television. I came here—I was actually on my way to Chicago for about a month or so. Before I left, I came down here because I heard about the seven hundred arrests on Brooklyn Bridge. Then I heard about the Union Square pepper spray night. For some reason, something triggered in me. "I've really got to see what's going on there."

All my friends and my clients were like, "Don't go down there. You'll get arrested." I didn't have that fear. I just knew I needed to see what it was about because it was happening in my back yard.

So I came down here on a Friday night—I think it was the thirtieth of September—asked questions, went around ... I can't even say what happened. All I knew was I had to come back. I stayed in a hotel a couple of days because I gave up my apartment. I stayed for three days in a hotel to decide, "Do I really want to come back here, or do I want to head back home to figure out my own situation?" I decided, "You know what? Let me come back here on Monday and see how it is." So I slept here Monday, and I've been here ever since.

I said to myself, "The day it feels like something that I don't believe in—which is being a total anarchy/violence movement—I'm out. If I don't see a good in it—I don't see a potential in it, a hope in it—I'm going back." And you know, I haven't taken a project in a month, and I have three more months of work. I get into the union—the hair and makeup union—which is very important to me because it means I get my benefits, and I get to actually be working on films like the Batman film that's here right now.[2] Right now I work on indie films. So I have been putting that off. It's a little bit stressful because I know I need to get back to work—I really need my own situation—but it's so hard to leave because I see it grow every day.

When I give up hope, then all of a sudden a new group is coming up with something that I thought, "Oh, man! I was just thinking we need that!" So I just see it growing every day, and every day it's harder to extricate myself. I feel like I want to be a part of it. I want to be here when we get that ... well, what I'm hoping is we get a message to our leaders that we voted into office—who are making our laws for us and working for us—saying, "We want a public discourse with y'all, and we want to show you what changes we are now going to make." That's what I want to see. Will it happen? You know, will money be out of politics any time soon? No, but I want to see a big push towards that. I want to see an inkling of that before I leave.

We see that in the little ways. We have a lot of diligent people who are part of what they call the one percent. They don't have to check the bank accounts; they have the money to offer. They have the donations, they have the heart, and they are believing in this. When I see that, it's like, "Yeah, those are the people who have the contacts with the politicians and the lawmakers, who have the influence with them, who know them, who have dinner with them." That they're on our side is sort of an inkling towards opening up that public discourse.

---

[2] *The Dark Knight Rises*, directed by Christopher Nolan (Burbank, CA: Warner Bros. Pictures, 2012).

Let's make changes for our society. Let's not say we have no money for keeping the mentally ill in institutions. Let's say we do have the money. Let's find a way to get them the help they need. Let's find a way to keep Social Security and medical benefits. Let's find a way to get better-paying jobs. People have these terribly low-wage incomes. They're struggling to keep their heads above water, barely able to get work, barely able to pay for the MetroCards, you know, because they have a family. I'm single, I make good money, and *I'm* struggling. It's a disgrace. Right now ... I think it's tomorrow, we have No Fares for the Unemployed. We have that going on. I want to see that!

Oh, I think that's great!

Isn't it, Olivia?

I think that's great.

Thank you!

Those are the inklings of hope that I see. When I give up hope, and I see something like that, I'm like, "Okay, I can stay a little longer. I can help to keep the movement here, and keep pushing that along, and keep other people coming here, and encouraging other people."

ॐ

A lot of my friends and family don't even know that I'm here. Of course,

my parents do, but . . . Clearly, everybody knows that the occupation is here. I mean, it's been fifty-something ... what? Fifty-two days about now? Everybody knows we're here, so I don't want to force it down anybody's throat. My clients, who some are the one percent—not necessarily my family members—I want them to ask me what it's about. I want them to come with an understanding before I present it to them.

For instance, I have a very, very good friend who's husband is a banker. They're not necessarily the one percent, but she had no idea that I've been down here all this time. She didn't even know I gave up my apartment to be here, and she's been a dear friend of mine for fifteen years. She's very successful.

We had dinner and we talked about it, and it was interesting to see her viewpoint because she was initially very angry, not knowing about me being here. So that's why I'm saying I don't really talk to people until I know that they want to talk about it. It's a bit of a delicate matter. Like, my friend ... when she allowed me to talk about it, I engaged in a conversation, and I could say she left with more of an understanding of what it's about. She just heard all these negative things like you and I are talking about in the media and the press. She just thought it was no system; just terrible, like, a bunch of homeless idealists and hippies.

And then she knew I was here, and she knows that that's not me. She knows I have never done this kind of thing, but she does know me as this friend who—I'm not a traditional kind of girl, you know? Some educated people work in the corporate world, and some educated people have chosen not to work in a corporate world, and I guess that's what I meant about my friends and myself. They know that I'm a little bit more of that kind of a free spirit type of person. I haven't finished college and I don't work in an office. I'm more of an artist.

It was nice to engage her, and it was nice to put that word out. Slowly, I'm getting to my friends, to my family. I guess my point in saying this is: We have still got a ways to go because even within my own self—my personal self—my friends and family still need some education on this, still need some dialogue on this, and still need some awareness. We still have a long way to go, but we do have Outreach, and it's helping along the way.

Personal outreach as well as reaching out to strangers.

Absolutely. I just—for me personally, I just don't want someone to engage negatively, because it's such a sensitive issue right now. It's very difficult mentally and physically to sleep out here. I'll be honest, six days I slept in a hotel because my friend had a hotel room. One day I got really sick, and I slept at a friend's house. But I feel more connected sleeping here because then I understand what it takes to make a stand here. Where to wash up, where to go to the bathroom, what we need in terms of winterizing, and being here in Comfort. When you disconnect with that, then you disconnect a little bit with the movement.

Is there anything else that you would like to add?

People are really putting their blood, sweat and tears into this. That's what I would really like to tell people. There's a lot of blood, sweat and tears from a lot of beautiful people. It's pretty great. It's pretty amazing. It's pretty amazing to be part of it, just to be part of it.

I feel very fortunate, even though some days you'll see me losing my cool, like, "Aagh!" I lose my cool when people put us down. Like, "Oh, yeah? Well, you don't have this? Nice going!" Okay, well, our legal team is not here because it's one a.m. Our press are not here because it's two a.m. We don't have the information for you because it's three a.m. and I just got off Community Watch. We haven't cleared the pathways because we can't account for people who come in and . . .

When people do that, you'll see me losing my cool. You will see me losing my cool. ❧

Congratulations!
You're part of the problem!

Were you among that group of city dwellers who avoided the park at Wall Street in 2011 because of your abhorrence of homeless individuals?

Are you the sort who turns up your nose at crusty punks?

Did you think that that was the only sort of person who was down at Liberty Plaza? And if it had been, would you consider questioning your preconceptions about the worth of human individuals? No? Oy, for Pete's sake!

Well, now look what you bought yourself! You might have redeemed your politics five years ago, but instead, by ignoring what was going on, you have a demagogue for a president and a nation of disenfranchised and angry people. Couldn't we have done something to stop this then?

Buy this book and try to get a grip on yourself!

Ballpoint Perps!

Oct. 24

Michael
Age 25
Resisting an
   officer w/out
Viol (obstruction),
Felon in possession

of Firearm,
Carrying concealed
Firearm,
Resisting an
Officer with
Violence
   P.O.B. NY